THE CREATION OF AN ARTIST

Grant Wood's Boyhood Story

Barbara Feller

Ice Cube Press, LLC
North Liberty, Iowa, USA

THE CREATION OF AN ARTIST:
Grant Wood's Boyhood Story

First Edition

ISBN 9781948509183

Library of Congress Control Number: 2020938261

Ice Cube Press, LLC (Est. 1991)
1180 Hauer Drive
North Liberty, Iowa 52317 USA
www.icecubepress.com | steve@icecubepress.com

The paper used in this publication meets the minimum requirements of the American National Standard for Information Sciences—Permanence of Paper for Printed Library Materials, ANSI Z39.48-1992.

Manufactured in USA

Note on Cover: In her 2020 book, *Grant Wood's Secrets*, art historian and author, Sue Taylor, suggests that *Spring in the Country,* shows Grant Wood's memory of himself helping his mother set out cabbage seedlings while his father plows with a team of horses on the rise behind them.

Dedicated to Bob Kocher who, as the Marvin Cone Professor of Art at Coe College, 1959-1995, was responsible for the creation of many artists.

Author's notes

Creation of an Artist is almost entirely based on Grant Wood's own words and art. Early events were dictated to his secretary, Park Rinard, in an incomplete and therefore unpublished autobiography, *Return from Bohemia*. Others were mentioned in letters Wood wrote as a ten-year-old boy, just after moving to Cedar Rapids. Most of the rest of the story is taken from memories shared by Nan Wood Graham in books *Grant Wood and Little Sister Nan* and *My Brother, Grant Wood* by Julie Jensen McDonald.

The prologue is a story handed down through Grant Wood's family and presented in Darrell Garwood's 1944 biography, *Artist in Iowa*. It introduces readers to Wood's extended conflict between his father's expectations and his own interests in art. Apocryphal or not, I decided this story is a perfect introduction to my theme.

Happy reading!

Barbara Feller
June, 2020

Prologue

When their second son was born on February 13, 1891, Hattie and Francis Maryville Wood named him Grant after the great Civil War general.

For a middle name, the parents chose De Volsen in honor of the infant's maternal grandfather.

The red, round, and wrinkled baby squalled worse than a winter storm in Iowa if anyone tried to take him from his mother's arms. This made his father very happy. "It's good to have him spirited and chunky," he said. "He'll grow up to be a fine, strong farmer that way."

"He certainly is a tough little fighter," Clarabelle Weaver said smiling bravely over her tiny cousin's flailing fists. "But I think you'd better let me take charge of him for now or Cousin Hattie may never have a chance to eat!"

Clarabelle pulled the baby closer to her shoulder and began marching back and forth across her well-furnished parlor. Pretty soon, the entire family was gratified with silence.

"Is he asleep?" Hattie asked. "However did you manage him?"

"See for yourself," Clarabelle replied.

Baby Grant De Volsen Wood wasn't sleeping at all. Instead, his gaze was firmly fixed on a framed work of art hanging on the parlor wall.

"I think we have a budding artist on our hands," the baby's cousin whispered.

Chapter 1

Father was dead.

Ten year old Grant Wood knew that, of course. Even so, Grant still expected to pass his father's tall, gaunt figure leaning over a horse and plow whenever he and Frank made their way down the familiar lane.

Grant didn't share these thoughts aloud. Instead, he and his older brother rode in silence. Once in a while, Frank stirred himself to brush a fly from the back of one of the horses with his whip. Other than that, their wagon's crawling progress seemed the only movement on the countryside this Saturday morning. The dust hung in thick clouds, especially as the boys passed through airless lanes where the road was shut in on both sides by corn.

It was uncomfortable, but Grant didn't mind. Their weekly trip to Anamosa was the single most restful time he and Frank had now that their father had died. Twenty cows to milk each morning and night; stables to be cleaned; sheep, hogs, and poultry to tend, didn't leave much time for fun. Ma still saved cardboard from cracker boxes and burnt chunks of firewood, since they had no money to purchase real art tools. But Grant hadn't used them for weeks. He simply had no time.

There was a kind of peacefulness to the ride, though. Insects screeched and clicked in the dusty road like they were playing in a crazy rhythm band. Coarse leaves of drying corn whispered in the breeze. The occasional snorting of the horses, the clip-clop of their hoofs, and the metallic clanking of the milk cans he and his brother were hauling to town, played like a lullaby. So, as was his habit, Grant let Frank do the driving while he yielded to the swaying farm wagon and memorized details he might later draw from the scenes around him.

On this day, the landscape seemed a patch-work quilt of bleached yellow grains, forest-green squares of pasture, and light green meadows. Glorious colors, he thought.

As they turned out of their lane, Grant saw their neighbor repairing his fence.

"Hello, Mr. Abbott," Frank shouted, slowing the horses.

"Hello there! How are you boys getting along running the farm?"

"Just fine!" Frank called.

Grant's response was not as enthusiastic. "We're okay," he said.

With less than a mile's difference separating their two farms, the Abbots had been the Wood's closest friends for as long as Grant could remember. Mrs. Abbott and Ma shared recipes, gardening tips, and even bits of gossip. Grant realized how important these little communications were for Ma. But seeing Mr. Abbott only reminded him of the day his father had forced the boys to return the book of *Grimms' Fairy Tales*.

"It was kind of Mrs. Abbott to loan the book to you and you should thank her. But tell her we Quakers can only read true things," Father had instructed.

Frank turned onto a smoother road. As the horses gathered speed, Grant's thoughts returned to art. The leaves would be turning soon. He should collect some. When he had time, he could draw them. How could he reproduce autumn golds and oranges? Maybe mix some clay into juices from Ma's berries? No, that might make the colors too muddy…

"See that clearing over there?" Frank said, as if Father had alerted him that Grant was daydreaming again. "That's where I had to jump when a horseless carriage came by last week."

Grant looked up. "Gee, I wish I'd been with you," he said.

"You never heard such a racket in all your life. I bet you would have been scared!"

"Would not!" Grant protested.

"Oh sure you would. I remember the times you woke me in the night because you thought our haystacks were Indian braves out on the attack..."

"That's not fair! I was only a little kid then."

The argument came to a halt when the boys spotted a wagon coming their way.

"Must be a stranger," Frank said. "Nobody around here has a rig like that."

The approaching driver appeared to be an elderly man with a long gray beard. When he got nearer, he reined the horses over to the side of the road and stopped.

"Grandfather Weaver!" the two boys shouted in one voice.

Grandfather greeted them with a huge smile.

"What a nice surprise. I'm up here to visit your ma, see how she's gettin' along. Grandmother had to stay home, so I came from Cedar Rapids by myself. Took the train to Anamosa and rented this here rig and mare from the livery there. Ain't they dandy?"

Grant reached over and petted the horse.

"She's a beauty for sure," he said.

"Elegant rig, too," Frank added. "It's almost as modern looking as a horseless carriage."

"You rather like those fancy new contraptions, don't you Frank?" Grandfather said with a grin.

Frank nodded.

"Well, better be on my way. I suppose you boys will be back on the farm in time for dinner. I'll see you then," Grandfather said, clucking at his horse. "Be careful now!"

"Ma will sure be surprised," Frank said after the rig was out of sight.

"I'll say! Do you suppose Grandfather remembered to bring us anything from the city?"

"Of course he did. Can't wait to see what it is!"

Chapter 2

It was close to 5:00 by the time the boys arrived home. Grant fed Dewey, whose excited bark had followed him from the time they'd pulled into the farm lane.

Frank got Pat unhitched and settled into the stable for the night.

"Dinner's ready," Ma called from the porch stoop. "Don't worry about your other chores yet. We've got company!"

The two boys quickly splashed water on their hands and faces from a wooden trough near the cistern and hurried into the house. Their younger brother, Jack, was already seated at the dining room table. Baby Nan was in her high chair, and the table was set with Ma's best china.

Grandfather Weaver was sitting in Father's chair at the head of the table, tugging at his beard, a sure sign he was concentrating on something important. Frank and Grant glanced at each other as they took their places.

"Grandfather brought us candy," Jack shouted. "Three whole boxes for us to share!"

"That's all very fine," Ma said. "But Grandfather has something important to say to you."

Grandfather began speaking only after Ma had finished serving and prayers of thanks had been said.

"Your mother tells me you have been doing a good job of taking care of the farm, better than could be expected," he began. "That's fine. We're proud of you. And the work won't hurt you none, either. It will do you good, in fact.

"But pretty soon school will be starting. You won't be able to do all the chores and go to school too. And your ma says that whatever happens, she's going to see that you go on with your studies."

"Your father had dreams you boys might even attend college one day," Ma said in a quiet voice.

"Now you could stay here on the farm and try to get on the best you can. You'd have to hire help and a good man is hard to find. Besides, you can't afford one," Grandfather continued.

Grant nodded. He knew they didn't have much money. Only last year a Cedar Rapids newspaper had advertised a drawing contest for children. He'd worked a steady two days in preparation but his hopes were dashed the moment his father stepped down from the wagon after his weekly trip to Anamosa.

"I'm sorry, son," he'd said. "The smallest bottle of India ink was 25 cents. We simply can't afford it."

Grandfather was still speaking. "…so it just don't look like you'll be able to keep up payments on the farm. Your ma and me discussed all these things. We finally hit upon a plan but your ma said she wanted to see how you boys felt before she made up her mind. So now it's up to you: How would you like to move to Cedar Rapids?"

"Yes!" all three boys shouted.

Chapter 3

Ma lost no time. She inserted ads in the *Anamosa Eureka* and, within a week, several prospective buyers turned up.

The *Anamosa Journal Eureka* has been in Anamosa since 1855.

By the middle of August the farm was sold. The move to Cedar Rapids became a certainty.

"Is Cedar Rapids really bigger than Anamosa?" Jack asked over and over.

"Anamosa!" Frank snorted. "Why Cedar Rapids' little finger is bigger than Anamosa."

The three boys could think of nothing else. Anamosa was the largest town Jack and Grant had ever visited, but Frank had actually been to Cedar Rapids. He'd made the trip shortly after Grandfather and Grandmother Weaver moved there. His accounts of the city were glowing. His description of a modern bathroom had been especially vivid:

"Instead of privies, you just go do it right in the house. You pull a chain and there is a tremendous gurgling sound…"

The people who were buying the farm wanted the Wood family to leave by the first week in September. Ma felt that didn't give them enough time to prepare.

"We can ship all the household goods to Cedar Rapids, but how can we sell the livestock and farm implements in that short amount of time?" she fretted.

"You'll have to auction the stuff," Grandfather Weaver proclaimed on his next visit.

"Auction!" Grant shouted in an excited voice. He'd always wanted to go to an auction. Now one was coming to him.

Grandfather Weaver went to work arranging things. Poster papers called dodgers were printed in Anamosa. Within a few days the bright yellow, blue, and red signs advertising the sale of livestock and farm implements were plastered on trees, barn sides, and fence posts throughout Jones County.

"Ma, will all the cows be sold at the auction?" Grant asked during a short lull in the excitement.

"Yes, Son. We can't take them with us."

"The chickens too?"

Grant loved the chickens. He'd been gathering eggs and cleaning the hen house since he was five. Even though they didn't have names, he was able to recognize each hen by her markings. He especially remembered drawing a hen when he was about six. Father had criticized the number of eggs he'd drawn as being too many for one bird to lay. But the thrill he'd felt when Ma actually recognized it as a Plymouth Rock Hen made him feel he was a true artist.

"What about Pat?" he whispered after a pause.

"Pat's a grand horse for sure. None as gentle as him for riding or as strong for pulling a plow," Ma responded. "But I'm afraid he wouldn't be happy in the city."

"But Dewey will be okay in the city. He can come, right?" Grant's voice was getting shaky now. Father had bought the collie pup to replace old Shep three summers ago. Shep had been Frank's dog, but it was Grant who was given the responsibility of caring for Dewey.

"We'll see, Grant," Ma said in a tired voice. "We'll see what can be done about Dewey."

Chapter 4

Grant peered out the back door on the morning of the auction. The sky was overcast from a bad storm they'd had during the night.

Its grayness reminded him of the nightmarish clouds his mind had painted over Cedar Rapids as he'd tossed and turned imagining his new life in the city. Now that auction day was here, he wasn't so sure about this whole moving thing.

"Maybe no one will come," he said to himself, somewhat hopefully.

But, before chores were done, several mud-plastered wagons pulled into the farmyard, and a big crowd of farmers began milling about. A short time later the auctioneer arrived.

Dad Walters was a ruddy, stub-legged little man with a droopy, tobacco-stained mustache that wiggled when he smiled. Jack and Grant, with Dewey at their heels, ran to meet him.

"Well lookie here," he bellowed from high on his wagon seat. "Durned if there ain't a welcome committee. Hey there boys!"

The brothers helped unhitch the auctioneer's old nag, a strawberry roan Mr. Walters claimed was the best horse in Jones County, Iowa. They put it out to pasture and tagged after the auctioneer as he marched right up to the kitchen door greeting the farmers and families he passed along the way.

"Good morning, Hattie!" he shouted when he reached Ma. "Thought I'd gossip with you a few minutes before the sale begins."

The brothers watched the auction from seats on the back porch steps.

"This is exciting stuff!" Frank exclaimed.

"Mmm," Jack nodded, his mouth full of cookies.

Grant watched in silence, his mind's eye as focused as the lens of a camera. Mr. Walters kept things moving fast. The farm implements and all the hogs were sold before noon.

The crowd gobbled down the towering stacks of hogshead cheese sandwiches Mrs. Abbott had prepared for lunch, making chomping noises that reminded Grant of pigs at the trough. He'd always hated those pigs; thought they were the rudest animals on the farm. Now they'd been sold and he wasn't going to miss them at all. But after lunch, as he watched sheep, cows, turkeys, and the Plymouth Rock hens sell like vegetables at a farmers' market, Grant's stomach began to feel queasy. When he was asked to lead Pat up and down the lane in front of the crowd, he put on a brave face, but thought he might actually throw up.

Grant returned to the porch steps after the ordeal.

Ma came up to him. She looked happier than he'd seen her in days. Relief showed in her eyes as she spoke.

"Pat brought us a whole $50. And, guess what Grant?" she said. "Mr. Cheshire, who bought him, offered a home for Dewey too! His dog died recently and he needs a good herder."

"You mean Dewey's not coming with us?" Grant choked on the words.

"Dewey and Pat will be together in the same home," said Ma. "Isn't that wonderful?"

Hearing his name, Dewey came up and nuzzled against Grant.

"It's going to be okay, boy," Grant whispered, stroking the dog.

He only wished he could believe it.

Chapter 5

A busy week of preparation flew by after the auction. Now it was Saturday, moving day. Dewey's thumping tail woke Grant at dawn.

The dog had been permitted to sleep inside the house and was eager to begin his new day. Grant reached over from the bare mattress he'd been sharing with Jack on the floor of their bedroom.

"Good morning," he said, pulling the dog's furry warmth toward him.

Dewey licked his face in response.

"You want to go out, don't you, boy?" he said. "Come on. Let's go."

Grant tiptoed through the house. Dewey tagged along in silence as if he too noticed that the smallest sounds echoed in the empty rooms.

Ma was in the kitchen already. Same as always, but different, Grant thought. The breakfast plates were set out on packing boxes instead of the table.

"I'm glad you're up. We'll have to hurry like everything," Ma said. "I'd like you to check the barn and hen-house before Mr. Flynn arrives to take us to the station. We need to be sure we haven't left anything behind.

"Sure, Ma."

Grant knew there was little chance of anything being left behind after the week-long scrubbing and sweeping since the auction, but he was happy to get outside where he could collect lasting images to store inside his head.

The farm lay silent and deserted, like a country churchyard. No rooster crowed. No cows grazed in the yard, ready to be milked. No pigs were squealing for food, and no turkeys hung about waiting for their morning feed. The only sound was the steady whistling of the windmill and the rapid click of the pump shaft.

"It looks like ghosts are the only things being left behind," Grant whispered to Dewey.

When they returned to the kitchen, Jack and Frank were on the floor eating breakfast. Mrs. Abbott was there too. She had brought over a shoe box bulging with chicken sandwiches for eating on the train.

"Of course we'll come in to see you," she was saying, "provided I can ever budge that husband of mine to leave the farm for a day."

Grant shared his fried mush and graham gems with Dewey out on the back stoop. He was glad to see their little red grocery cupboard packed amongst several neat bundles of bedding and clothing. Father had made the sturdy house-shaped box, painted it red, and finished it off with an iron clasp for Ma. It still held a spicy smell from the jars and bottles of herbs that Ma had stored inside.

Graham Gems, a popular breakfast food in Grant Wood's day, are a type of muffin made from a base of graham flour mixed with sweet or sour milk.

Jack joined him carrying a great armload of cedar darts, toy windmills, and other home-made toys. "We'll need these when we get to Cedar Rapids," he said dumping them in an untidy pile.

Frank came out next, bounded down the porch steps, and ran down the lane.

"Ma, he's coming now. I see him. Better get ready, men," he shouted. "Mr. Flynn's heading our way."

Frank's call started a final whirlwind of confusion, but the friendly John Flynn confidently helped the family load their things onto his wagon. He tucked Jack, Grant, and Dewey into the front section of the wagon box. Mr. Flynn then took his place and helped Ma climb onto the wagon seat beside him. Frank handed baby Nan up to Ma, then took his own place at the back of the wagon to see that nothing fell off. They were on their way.

Chapter 6

Grant took one last look around as the wagon bumped and jolted its way down the familiar drive and over the small wooden bridge he had crossed so many times.

Tall weeds were growing in Ma's garden. The onions and lettuce had gone to seed. The house was even worse. Without curtains, it looked like a man without any eyelids. Grant turned away in sadness. He had no wish to remember these scenes.

Cottonwood School was named for the trees that formed a semi-circle in front of it. Known by its formal name, Antioch, the one room school is now a museum.

The Cottonwood School was closed, but Grant recognized a lone figure splitting wood in the schoolhouse yard as one of the Byerly brothers. The boy stopped his work to wave; then watched them go by. Grant felt as if he should be there, somehow, even though it was a Saturday. When the wagon started up Cheshire Hill, Grant's throat tightened. Dewey was to be left here.

"Don't look like anybody's home," said John Flynn, as he stopped in front of the farm.

A wave of Ma's hand indicated Grant was to go anyway. He climbed out of the wagon and trudged up the drive. Faithful Dewey trotted along by his side. The barnyard was empty.

"Hello!" Grant shouted.

No answer. The house was locked up and the wagon was gone. Grant shot a pleading look toward Ma. She only shook her head and pointed toward the barn.

Grant unhooked the door and entered the silent space with Dewey following at his heels. When they reached the center of the darkness, Grant turned, ran out of the barn, banged the door shut behind him, and hurried back to the wagon.

Mr. Flynn urged his team up the remaining few yards to the top of the road in silence.

"At least we won't have to struggle up and down this hill anymore," Ma said, trying to break the gloom.

Then Mr. Flynn called out, "Look there!"

They all jerked their heads forward. A big white horse was galloping up the road, top speed, its rider low over its neck.

"Lord he's riding fast. Wonder what's wrong," Frank said.

For a moment it looked as though horse and rider were going to plunge into a ditch when suddenly the stranger pulled his mount short.

"President McKinley is dead!" the rider yelled. Then, turning quickly, he disappeared in a cloud of dusty road.

"The president died? Last Sunday, our pastor told us President McKinley had been shot," said Mr. Flynn, "but we all expected him to live."

"My teacher told us if something happens to the president, then the vice president takes over," Frank said.

"You're right my boy," Mr. Flynn responded. "Mr. Theodore Roosevelt is probably already sworn in as president."

"Lincoln, Garfield, and now McKinley," Ma whispered. She buried her face against baby Nan, gave a sudden gasp, and began sobbing.

Mrs. Wood was referring to former U.S. presidents who had been assassinated: President Lincoln in 1865, John Garfield in 1881 and now William McKinley in 1901.

Chapter 7

Grant's concerns about Dewey vanished in the instant Ma's tears began. He'd never seen Ma cry before, not even at Father's funeral.

Ma had always been the strong one. But now she seemed like a little girl who was lost and afraid. Grant rose to his knees in the wagon and patted her shuddering shoulders.

Jack looked up. "We're still going to move, right?" he asked. "We're still to ride on a train?"

Grant nodded. Jack crawled over and snuggled next to him. "I'm scared of the train," he whimpered. "It's going to be noisy!"

"The noise can't hurt us," Grant soothed, putting a protective arm around his little brother. Jack's lower lip trembled.

"Remember how we pretended the threshing machines were fire-eating dragons?" Grant whispered. "I'll bet the train will be just like them."

"Really?"

"Sure! And they never hurt us, did they?"

"No," Jack agreed.

Grant pulled his little brother closer and stared out over the familiar fields of corn. Like the little flip books he'd seen at the general store in Anamosa, scenes began flashing through his mind.

There were the threshers, who came every year. Ma and Mrs. Abbott and other women spent a full day preparing dinner for the hard working men. And there was that hard patch of soil where nothing grew. Father had explained that this was a buffalo wallow, caused by the gathering of the large beasts who'd pounded out their territory hundreds of years before it became part of the Woods' pasture.

The wind carried the scents of drying autumn leaves and wild flowers, reminding him of the time Miss Linden had asked him to gather up plants that grew around the schoolhouse and draw them so that he and his classmates could study nature even in winter.

Grant looked down at his little brother, who was now asleep. You're not the only one who is afraid, he thought. As they neared the station, he heard the distant whistle of an approaching train. Their future was coming.

Chapter 8

The Union Depot was a full city block in length. It had an elegant gabled roof and walls made of golden Stone City stone.

Grant thought it looked more like the country home of a king than an ordinary train station.

Mr. Flynn drew his horse alongside several other wagons just as their approaching train was announced. Grant, Frank, and Jack ignored any unloading that was to be done, jumped out, and immediately ran to the platform. A deafening burst from the train's whistle sent Jack running, but Grant stood firm even when he felt the ground shake and heard the piercing squeal of brakes that declared the train's thundering arrival.

"Just look at that engine," Frank gloated, as if he had made the machine himself. "It's powerful enough to pull 15 tons."

Grant stared in awe. The engine truly was a monster. Its wheels alone were taller than the engineers who ran it!

"First train you've seen up close?" asked Mr. Flynn, who had joined them unnoticed.

"Sure is, sir," Grant replied. "We've seen 'em plenty of times across the other side of the creek, but never close up."

"Well, you boys better help me unload. It's a half hour before the train leaves but time's sure to go by quick as a wink."

Grant felt a shiver of excitement at the idea that he'd actually be riding a train in just half an hour! As he turned away he noticed a man loading bundles from the train to a uniformed platform workman who then piled them on a flat railway cart.

"Hey, boys!" he called. "If you need this here wagon, just give us a shout. Soon as we're done it's yours."

"Sure, thanks, sir!" Frank shouted.

"You two go get it," Frank said, pulling Jack out from behind a square corner column where he'd been hiding. "Mr. Flynn and me'll help Ma and baby Nan."

Grant and Jack dragged the heavy cart over to the farm wagon.

"Somehow Nan slept through all that noise," Ma said, shaking her head. "Sure wish I could feel that calm."

"She does have the right idea there, Mrs.Wood," said Mr. Flynn.

"Hello. Name's Lacock, Chief Engineer here," said the man who'd offered the flat rail wagon. "Ever been on a train, Ma'am?"

"No, nor my boys neither." A worried frown creased Ma's forehead.

"Ma, no need to fret. Trains are just about the finest invention there is," Frank insisted. "Why Cedar Rapids is a full twenty-five miles away but it will only take us two hours to get there!"

"Is it safe to go so quickly?" Ma asked.

"You don't have to worry none," said Mr. Lacock. "Your boy's right. Iowa trains carry tons of livestock and grains all year round. We feed the nation. And there hasn't been an accident here since March."

Grant felt a lurch in his stomach at this news.

"It was a pretty good one, too," Mr. Lacock continued in a cheerful voice. "No one was hurt, Ma'am. Several coal cars derailed, but they was right next to the depot's coal shed so we just swept the coal on in and used it for ourselves!"

Mr. Flynn laughed.

"But time's a wasting," said Mr. Lacock. "If you folks want to catch that train of yours, we better get packing!"

With that, Mr. Lacock, Mr. Flynn, and Frank took over. Minutes later, with bundles safely tucked in overhead shelves, the Wood family was seated in their coach, their tickets were punched, and good-byes said to Mr. Flynn. With a sudden jolt, the train headed forward. The ride to Cedar Rapids had begun!

Chapter 9

The benches, the walls, and even the curved ceiling inside the railway car were made of highly polished slats of wood.

The seats, which were placed back to back, were connected with black enameled wrought iron. All this reminded Grant of the frames that connected the benches to school desks back at Cottonwood School.

Grant sat next to Ma, who held his still-sleeping baby sister on her lap. His two brothers sat facing them; Jack with a rather silly-looking grin on his face, and Frank who couldn't seem to stop talking.

"See those men over there with their pocket watches out?" Frank asked as the train began moving. "That one is the station master. The one next to him is the engineer. They have to match up the time on their watches with the station clocks to be sure we're on schedule."

How did Frank know all these things? Grant wondered.

As the train picked up speed, the rhythmic sounds of wheels against track seemed to sooth Ma. She was soon nodding off. So Grant pushed Frank's chatter to the back of his mind and stared out the window. He pretended the window was a picture frame and he was in some sort of huge museum where all he had to do was sit while the paintings moved alongside him.

The first "painting" he saw looked like a castle. A sign told him it was no castle, though. It was the Anamosa State Penitentiary. He'd heard of that place. It was filled with killers. One had killed his own mother when he was only 10 years old!

Grant Wood would make Stone City, Iowa famous for the art colony he directed there in the summers of 1932 and 1933.

As the train headed out of town, they passed a huge farm with buildings made of stones from Stone City. Pa had told him the convicts worked right out here in the open. What if one of them managed to escape? What if he hopped on this very car? Grant gave a shiver.

He recognized the next scene, a cemetery. This was even worse. Maybe this wasn't such a good idea, Grant mused.

"That's where your Pa is buried," Ma whispered, as if she'd awakened in time to say one last good-bye. Grant huddled close to her. Frank stopped talking. Even Nan let out a whimper.

"Well!" Ma broke the silence a short time later as they passed over the Wapsipinicon River. "We can't let Mrs. Abbott's chicken sandwiches go to waste, now can we?"

"Cookies too?" asked Jack. "I'm hungry!"

Grant jumped up to pull the basket of food down from a shelf over their heads.

Ma offered a prayer of thanks as Grant distributed the sandwiches and handed a cookie to Nan.

"Da Da!" she said with a serious little face.

Grant knew that Nan was just making sounds. But somehow she made him feel grown up. And when he saw how the simple words brought tears to Ma's eyes, he decided he'd take special care of both Ma and baby Nan from now on.

Chapter 10

Grant couldn't sleep. He climbed out of bed, tiptoed over to the window, opened it, and looked out upon the scene.

The phonograph was developed in 1877 by Thomas Edison.

The night sky held the familiar patterns of stars, but gas lamps along the street reminded him he was in the city. He found himself listening to the faint tinkling of a neighbor's phonograph and horses clomping along the bricked streets of their neighborhood. These sounds were becoming familiar to him, but not comforting.

Several weeks after their arrival in Cedar Rapids, the Woods had moved from a rented house into this, their permanent new home. Grandfather Weaver had helped Ma find it. It was affordable, he'd said, and in a nice neighborhood.

They'd all trooped down to take a look. Grant liked it immediately because it included a small barn. He actually missed some of the old chores and thought maybe, with a barn, they might raise chickens again or even buy a cow.

Ma liked the fact that it included enough land for a nice sized vegetable garden. "This is fine! I can plant it up, come spring," she'd said in the most cheerful voice Grant had heard since Father died.

So, with a little help from Grandfather Weaver, the insurance Father had left them, and money from the auction and sale of their farm, Ma purchased it. The well-built "box" house with three bedrooms was on Fourteenth Street in a Cedar Rapids district known as Central Park.

Grant's mother used money from insurance and the sale of the farm to purchase the home at 318 14th Street NE Cedar Rapids. It can been seen to this day.

Grandfather Weaver dropped in almost every day to ask how things were going. Ma's reply was always, "We're getting by."

Grant wasn't exactly sure what this phrase meant, but he couldn't help worrying. Conversations between Ma and Grandfather frequently turned to whispers about money. And, when they ended there was always a kind of sadness behind Ma's smiles.

Then there was school. Grant was in the fourth grade at Polk Elementary School, which was only a couple of blocks from their new home. Uncle Clarence, Ma's brother, had tried to help by purchasing "city clothes" for him to wear. But the long pants, vest, and white shirt with a big bow tie made Grant feel ridiculous. Besides, the other boys weren't dressed that way at all. They wore tight-legged knee pants and turtle-neck sweaters. (Insert Photo)

"Whatcha doing? Is it morning already?" Jack murmured from the big bed they shared.

"No, I just couldn't sleep," said Grant. He turned away from the window, crawled back in under the quilt, and stared up through the darkness.

"Don't you like it here?" Jack whispered.

"I don't know," Grant said. "Most things are okay, I guess. I even heard they have a lady who comes around to teach art in school."

"I heard that too."

"But I'm clumsy in sports and I never know what to say to kids at recess."

"Me too," said Jack.

"I guess we were too busy with chores to play at sports back home," Grant said. "I mean, back on the farm."

"Mmmm," Jack agreed in a sleepy voice.

"And Ma seems so sad these days."

Hearing only gentle breathing, Grant realized his little brother had fallen back asleep. He stopped talking and traced shadows as they moved across the ceiling. There must be some way he could make things better, he thought. Grant tossed and turned for a good half hour before sleep finally came.

Chapter 11

"Grant, why aren't you dressed for school? Are you ailing?" Ma asked over breakfast the next morning.

"I'm fine," said Grant, "but city clothes are not for me."

"And shoes pinch," Jack added.

"I'll bet kids are razzing him," said Frank in his modern matter of fact way.

"Yesterday someone made fun of the big bow on Grant's shirt and asked if that was the way farmers dressed," Jack stated.

"Is that so, Grant? Do they make fun of you?" asked Ma. A worried frown showed upon her forehead when Grant nodded.

"They do me too," said Jack, "but I just swat at 'em and they shut up pretty quick."

"I can't fight 'em. I want to make friends, not enemies," said Grant, looking down at his plate of bacon and fried mush.

Frank turned to Grant. "What do you do then? Just run away?"

"No." Jack answered for his big brother. "He makes them laugh. Yesterday, he said if scarecrows wore this stuff, every bird in Jones County would have stayed away from our corn!"

Frank snorted.

Ma gave Frank her school-marm glare. She turned to Grant and said, "Once they get to know you, they'll be friends. I'm sure of it! You just be who God meant you to be."

Grant nodded sheepishly.

"I suppose it's all right for you to wear overalls, if that's what you like best," Ma added in a softer voice. "But it's much too cold to be barefoot. You go on upstairs. Put on shoes and those warm socks I knit you. We'll talk about this after school."

"Thanks, Ma." Grant scrambled up the stairs, happy he'd at least won part of his battle.

Grant kept his love of overalls his entire life. Children's biographer, John Duggleby used this fact when he chose the title of his 2005 children's biography: *Artist in Overalls: The Life of Grant Wood.*

Chapter 12

When all the students had taken their places in the warm, chalky-smelling classroom, Miss Wilson walked up to her desk on the raised platform in front.

"Good morning," she said. "I've planned a special surprise for you today. I'll tell you more as soon as we've recited the pledge."

The Pledge of Allegiance began on Columbus Day of 1892. Wording was revised in 1923 & 1924 with the phrase "Under God" added in 1954. Americans began covering the heart with the right hand in 1942 because the original was too similar to the Nazi salute.

It took a stern look from their teacher to quell the excited whispers of the children as they turned to face the American flag. Quieting down, they each stretched out their right arm, letting its palm face the floor, and recited: "I pledge allegiance to my flag and to the republic for which it stands: one nation indivisible with liberty and justice for all."

"Now children," Miss Wilson announced after they'd finished and sung America, "we're going to celebrate an early Bird Day. Our special activities will take place in two parts. In the morning we'll read about birds, learn a bit about their habits, and solve bird story problems in arithmetic."

Smiles all around.

"After lunch, Miss Grattan, the Cedar Rapids District Art Supervisor, will visit to give us lessons on drawing birds."

On May 4, 1894 Charles A. Babcock, Superintendent of schools in Oil City Pennsylvania created the first Bird Day. In Grant Wood's time the holiday was often celebrated in late spring along with Arbor Day

Grant sat up at attention.

Miss Wilson picked up a thick, green, leather volume with gold trim. The book was called *Citizen Bird*, she explained, and was filled with what she called charming stories told in the birds' own words.

Grant and his classmates folded their hands on their desk tops, faced front, and listened intently as their teacher began reading:

"A party of Swallows perched on the telegraph wires beside the highway where it passed Orchard Farm. They were resting after a breakfast of insects, which they had caught on the wing, after the custom of their family. As it was only the first of May they had plenty of time before nest-building, and so were having a little neighborly chat..."

Mabel Osgood Wright and Elliot Coues' book, *Citizen Bird*, "dedicated to all boys and girls who love birds and wish to protect them" was written in1897. It is now electronically available.

Grant found himself daydreaming. Orchard Farm could have been right outside Anamosa, he thought. He'd seen just such families of birds all the time back there. Suddenly Grant had another memory...one that got him very excited. Master Grant Wood could hardly wait for lunch time!

"You must be awfully hungry," Jack called to his brother a short time later when they were headed home for lunch. "I can't keep up with you!"

"Gotta get something at home." Grant gave no further explanation but continued his hurried pace.

When they reached home, Grant raced through the kitchen door, letting it slam shut right in Jack's face. He scrambled up the stairs, crawled under the eaves, and began rummaging through a still unpacked box that had been placed there.

"Found it!" Grant shouted as he galloped back downstairs.

"What are you talking about?" Ma asked. "You should be sitting down to eat lunch."

Grant waved a newspaper clipping in front of her face. "You must remember this, from the Anamosa Eureka!"

Ma took it and read aloud:

April 15, 1901. "Master Grant Wood, only ten years of age, reports that he has found 55 varieties of birds in this neighborhood. His communication on this subject is very interesting and shows that he is an observing, thoughtful, wide awake boy."

"Of course I remember it, but what is this all about?" Ma asked.

"Miss Wilson said today was Bird Day and I can tell about the birds I used to see and we're going to have an art teacher come and I can draw them and, and…"

Ma smiled.

"Can't we please eat now?" asked Jack.

Chapter 13

The newspaper clipping in his pocket gave Grant a new sense of confidence. He slid into his seat well before the bell, eager to begin his very first art class.

"Boys and girls, I'd like to introduce Miss Grattan, our District Art Supervisor. Please give Miss Grattan your full attention," Miss Wilson announced.

"Good afternoon, Miss Grattan," the children chimed in unison.

"Good afternoon, children," said the art teacher. "I am most happy to be here with you. Now, I ask, how many of you like to draw?"

Grant raised his hand high. He noticed that most of his classmates had raised theirs as well. He was happily surprised at this, as he didn't realize there would be that many.

"Have any of you ever tried drawing a bird?"

Fewer hands went up this time, but Grant's remained raised, his heart thumping in anticipation of Miss Grattan's next question. Would she ask what kinds of birds they'd noticed? Would he be able to share his newspaper?

"And do any of you have a favorite bird that you like to draw?" Miss Grattan continued. It wasn't quite the question he had anticipated, but Grant's hand shot up in a most enthusiastic way. "Yes, Master Wood?" she said, checking the seating chart Miss Wilson had provided. "Which type bird do you like drawing most?"

"Chickens, Ma'am!" Grant shouted in an uncharacteristically loud voice.

To his horror, the response produced quiet titters, laughter, and even a loud guffaw from one particularly strong boy who was always among the first chosen for teams at recess games.

"Always the farmer," someone said with a laugh.

"Class! That's quite enough," Miss Wilson admonished, tapping her desk with a ruler.

Grant slunk back in his seat and tried to hide. The sudden warmth flowing over his face, told him it had turned as red as his hair.

"That is a most delightful answer, young man," said Miss Grattan, as if she hadn't heard a sound from the others. "I, myself, believe chickens are almost the royalty of birds. Would you care to come up to the chalk board and share an example of your work?"

Caught between embarrassment and happiness at Miss Grattan's encouragement, Grant walked up to the front of the room. This was nothing like he'd imagined. He turned to the chalkboard and stood silently rocking from one foot to the other while he gathered details in his head. After several moments, he drew a Plymouth Rock Hen.

Grant wasn't quite sure why, but the class sat in silence as he worked. When he finished, he turned around and saw looks of amazement on their faces.

"That is wonderful. It's just a wonderful rendition," Miss Grattan enthused. "Look at the details, class. Master Wood even put his hen on a nest of eggs."

Then, a most astonishing thing happened. His classmates applauded.

Chapter 14

Grant practically flew down the street after school.
He couldn't wait to tell Ma about his day.

He doubled his speed when he saw that she was out in the yard talking to a neighbor.

"Grant," Ma called in a cheerful voice. "Come meet Mr. Lord. He has something to ask you."

"Hello young man! I've heard some very good things about you," said Mr. Lord, extending his right hand for Grant to shake. "I think your talents might lead to your earning some money. How would you like that?"

"Thank you sir," Grant stammered. He wondered how Mr. Lord could have already heard about his drawing.

"Yep! Your Ma tells me you are quite the farmer and I could surely use some help in that direction."

"Farmer?" Grant said, as if he'd never heard the word before.

"Well, not exactly a farmer, son," said Mr. Lord. "More a dairy man I guess."

Grant turned to Ma.

"Poor Grant," Ma said. "You look as confused as a chicken in a feather bed! Mr. Lord wants you to work for him."

"Yes, Grant. I'm sorry if we haven't been clear. You see, I have cows, right here in the city," said Mr. Lord. "And they need milking. But I also have another job. So I'd like to pay you to take care of them. You could begin as early as tomorrow morning."

Grant looked at Ma's smile of encouragement and suddenly understood that the sadness he'd noticed in her was due to money only in part. She also wanted her family to have friends and feel accepted in their new neighborhood.

So, Grant stood tall with a new determination and said, "Yes, sir. I'd be happy to help you out."

Chapter 15

The very next morning, Grant got up early enough to milk Mr. Lord's cows before breakfast.

The spaces between the houses he passed on his walk grew wider and larger until Grant realized, with some surprise, the neighborhood just beyond his home was really quite rural. No farms, of course, but he couldn't help noticing the grassy areas were almost large enough to be called pastures. The one right next to Mr. Lord's property even had a horse grazing on it.

When Grant returned for the second milking, just after school, the horse was so close to the fence surrounding the yard, that Grant knew he could actually touch her. He pulled an apple from a nearby tree to give the mare a treat.

Just then, an old man came hurriedly limping toward him.

"Hello," he called. "Don't go! I want to talk to you!"

Grant hid the apple behind his back.

"You must be Master Grant Wood," said the stranger, a bit out of breath. "Mr. Lord told me to be expecting you to show up 'round now. My name's Woitescheck."

Grant dropped the apple and reached out to shake hands.

"You planned on giving my little lady a treat?" Mr. Woitescheck asked, stooping to retrieve the apple.

Grant felt his face turn red. "Yyyes, sir," he mumbled.

"Oh, you can feed her all right son. I don't mind at all! In fact, I'd be glad if Petr makes a new friend."

"Did you say her name is Pat?"

"Almost. Her name is Petr, which is Czech for rock," said Mr. Woitescheck. "She's solid as a rock. Thought so right from the start. That's why I named her."

"We had a horse named Pat back on the farm. I kind of miss him," Grant said quietly stroking Petr's neck.

"Was your Pat also a rock?"

"No finer one for pulling a plow, Ma always said."

"Would you mind feeding and caring for my Petr?" asked Mr. Woitescheck. "I could pay you a bit if you would."

"Oh yes sir. I'd enjoy that!"

Grant knew this work would only confirm the idea that he was a farmer. But his earnings, small as they might be, would help the whole family. How could that be so bad? He said good-bye to his new employer, entered Mr. Lord's barn and pulled a little milking stool up close to the cow.

As he began milking, Grant continued to think. This little stool upon which he sat, the sound of the warm milk squirting into the pail, the sweet smell of hay, and now Petr the horse, brought comforting memories. There was also the sound of his class applauding his drawing. Grant smiled to himself. He could be both an artist and a farmer, a most happy combination.

Afterword

As a young student, Grant found lots of ways to connect his dreams with his school work.

When Miss Wilson read them a story about Christopher Columbus, he drew his vision of the Santa Maria and quietly placed it on her desk. At Thanksgiving, he drew turkeys. And, just for fun, he drew the head of a chicken on some brown packing paper and made his teacher a book cover.

By the following Christmas, when he drew a realistic Santa Claus descending a red brick chimney on the chalkboard, seemingly every child in Polk School had begun thinking of Grant Wood as an artist.

Recognizing his unusual talent, Miss Grattan encouraged Grant by providing him with paints and brushes so he could work on his art whenever he wished. Under Miss Grattan's guidance Grant progressed rapidly so that in 1905, his last year at Polk School, he won a national art prize. It was for a drawing of oak leaves submitted to the Eastern Crayon Company of New York.

Grant's reputation as a kind of agricultural handyman spread throughout the neighborhood, too. The painfully shy youngster turned the soil with a hand-plow, became known for raising and selling the earliest seed corn and tomatoes, and even mowing lawns.

Grant went from Polk to Washington High School where Miss Grattan introduced him to a fellow classmate who was also very interested in art, Marvin Cone. The two became fast friends. Their drawings, contributions to the yearbook, and designs of theater sets, earned respect of both students and faculty.

Recognition for their interest and talent resulted in the boys being given jobs unpacking and guarding works of art delivered to the Cedar Rapids Art Association, housed on the top floor of the public library opposite their school. In this way, both boys were inspired by their close contact with some of the top art works of the day.

By age 18, Grant knew he wanted to go to art school but he had very little money. One day, as he peered longingly into a life-drawing class at the University of Iowa, he saw an empty easel. Grant entered the studio, walked straight to that seat, sat down and began painting. When the teacher asked for his admission card, he said he had forgotten it. The teacher knew better, but was so impressed with Grant's work that she "forgot" to ask for the registration card ever again. Grant stayed for the entire year without being registered or paying.

Grant's first love was drawing and painting, but he and his family never had much money. Through necessity and years of hard work, Grant Wood became proficient in many practical lines. A born craftsman, he loved to work with all kinds of material. He experimented with carpentry, modeled figures out of clay, tried his hand at metal working, and learned the fundamentals of building and interior design.

Even at his peak, Grant never forgot his Iowa farm background, as this quote in the *New York Times* shows: "I lived in Paris a couple of years myself..." Wood remarked in 1936, "I learned that French painting is very fine for the French people and not necessarily for us. I realized that all the really good ideas I'd ever had come to me while I was milking a cow. So I went back to Iowa."

Grant never forgot his promise to care for his mother either. Both she and Nan shared his home, no matter how small, for the rest of their lives. In fact, Hattie Weaver Wood, Grant's mom, was the model and inspiration for his first successful painting, *Woman with Plants*, and sister Nan served as the model for the farmer's daughter in Wood's most famous painting of all, *American Gothic.*

Older brother Frank followed his passion for cars. While still a student in high school, a friend of the family offered Frank a ride home from school in the first "horseless carriage" in Cedar Rapids. The driver, their family friend, State Senator W.G. Haskell, helped Frank write to the company. The company sent a representative to meet with Grandpa Weaver. This resulted in Grandpa Weaver opening the first automobile dealership in Cedar Rapids in which Frank became full partner and little brother, Jack, a mechanic.

Eventually, Grant Wood made Iowa famous throughout the world by being a leader in what is called the Regionalist Movement of Art. Many schools in his home state of Iowa are named for him. And though his name may not be familiar outside Iowa, Grant Wood's most famous painting, *American Gothic,* has been called, by some, second only to Leonardo Da Vinci's Mona Lisa in fame. His paintings are featured in museums across the United States and his studio in Cedar Rapids is open for tours to this day.

In the end, Grant Wood rose from being an Iowa farm boy to become one of the world's most renowned artists. Grant Wood's is one of the great success stories of American life in the 20th century.

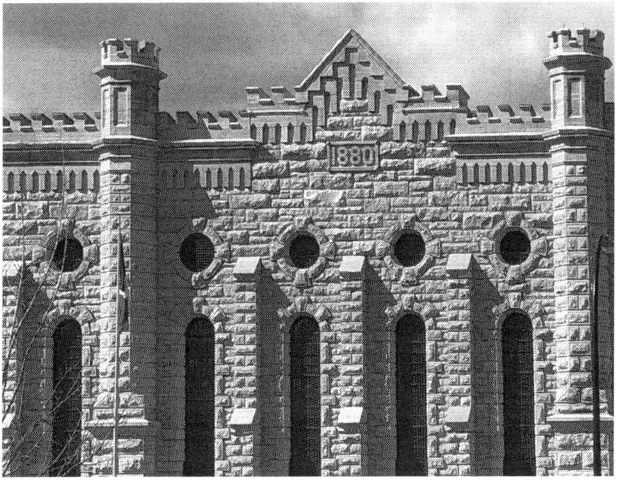

Stone City stone makes the Anamosa Prison look like a beautiful castle, but young Grant Wood had heard enough stories to be scared when the train passed by. Today's prisoners still grow and harvest and prepare meals from the crops on this farm.

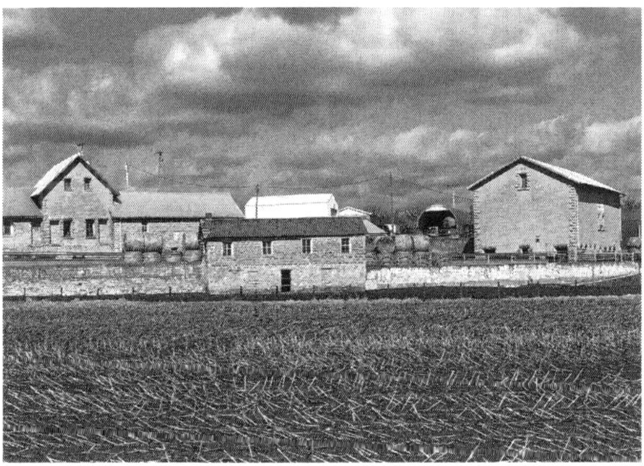

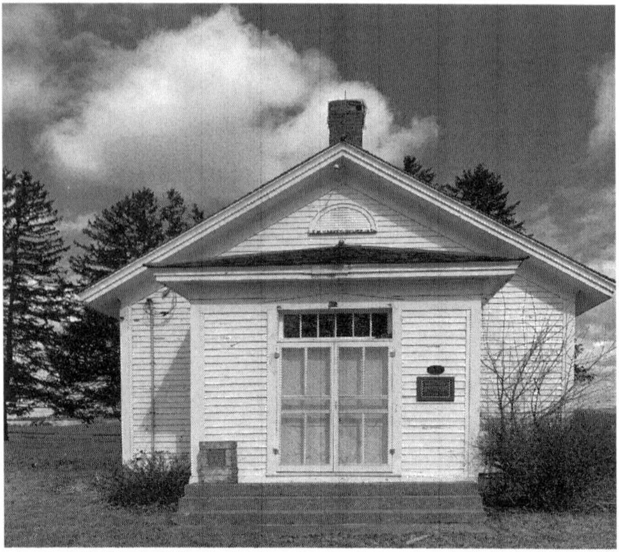

Antioch, the one-room schoolhouse known as Cottonwood School by the students in Grant Wood's day, is now a museum. Below: Sign on the school house museum. Photos by Steve Feller.

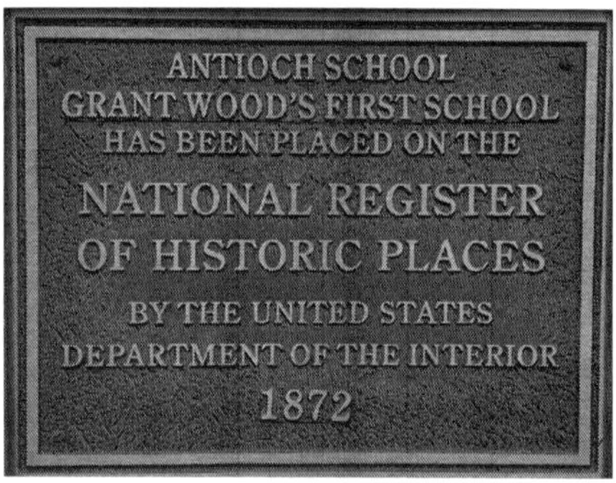

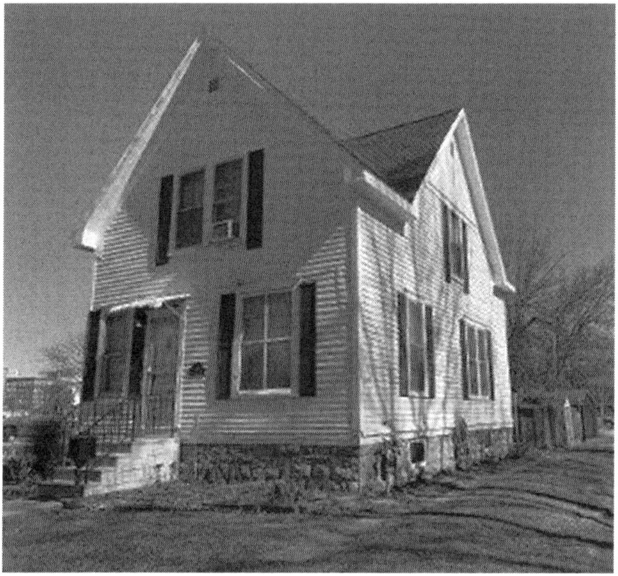

Grant Wood, his two brothers, baby sister and mother moved to this house, at 318 14th Street NE, Cedar Rapid in 1901. The garden his mother loved is still there. (Photo by Steve Feller.)

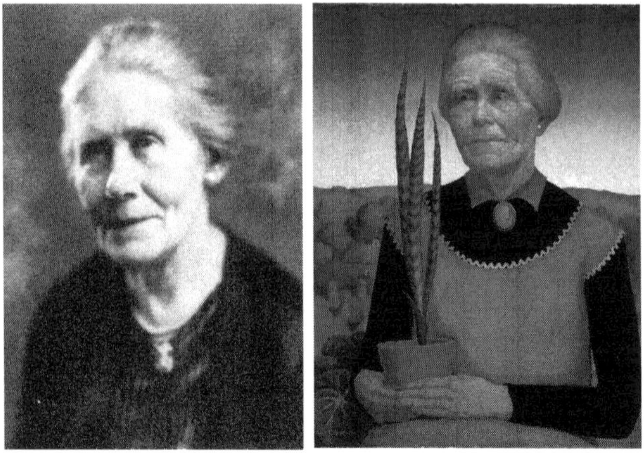

Left: Grant's mother, Hattie Weaver Wood as she looked in 1930. Right: Grant's painting, *Woman with Plants*.

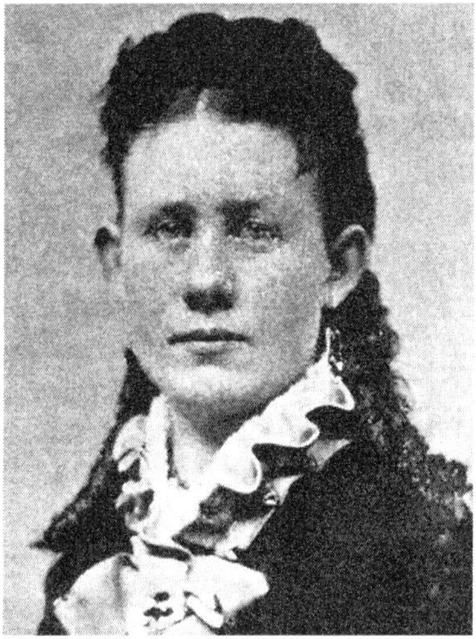

Hattie Weaver, Grant Wood's mother as she looked in 1874 just before she married his father.

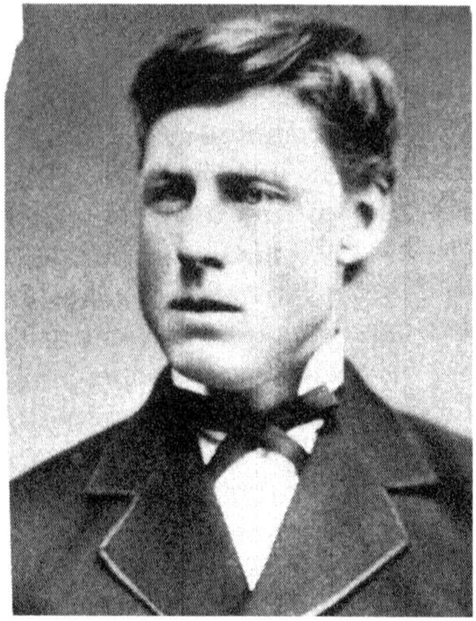

Francis Maryville Wood, Grant Wood's father.

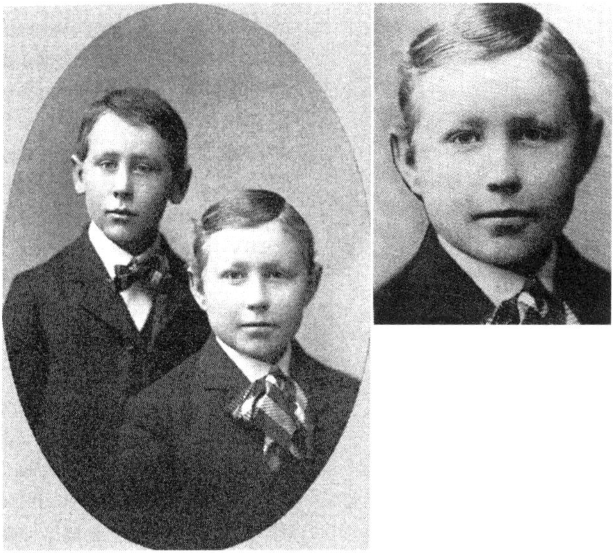

Grant's brother Jack, left, is 8 and Grant, right, is 10 in this picture. (Right, slightly enlarged image of Grant.)

Sources Used

Bliss, Perry, "The Death of a President," *Atlantic Monthly,* Volume 88, issue 527, September, 1901.

Brown, Hazel, *Grant Wood and Marvin Cone: Artists of an Era*, Iowa State University Press, Ames, Iowa, 1972.

Clements, Ralph, *Tales of the Town: Little Known Anecdotes of Life in Cedar Rapids*, Stamates Publishing Company, Cedar Rapids, Iowa, 1947.

Corn, Wanda, *Grant Wood: The Regionalist Vision*, Yale University Press, New Haven, 1983.

Duggleby, John, *Artist in Overalls: The Life of Grant Wood*, Chronicle Books 2005.

Floyd, David, *Railroads Come to Anamosa, in Anamosa 1838 – 1988: A Reminiscence*, Finn, Edited by Bertha Finn, Pat Worden Sutton, JoAnn McRoberts Walters, Mildred Barker Brown; The Montlcello Express, Monticello, IA, 1988

Garwood, Darrell, *Artist in Iowa: A Life of Grant Wood*, W.W. Norton & Company, New York, 1944.

Graham, Nan Wood, *My Brother Grant Wood*, State Historical Society of Iowa, 1993.

Graham, Nan Wood et al, *100th Anniversary of Antioch, Grant Wood's First School*, Pro Web Design, Anamosa Iowa, 1972.

Green, Edwin B., "Grant Wood of Iowa," *The Palimpsest: Iowa's Popular History Magazine*, Volume LIII (53), January 1972.

McDonald, Julie Jensen and Liffring-Zug, Joan, *Grant Wood and Little Sister Nan: Essays and Remembrances*, Penfield Press, Iowa City, Iowa, 2000.

Oxley, Marvin, *Cedar Rapids and Marion Railroad Consolidation, The History of Marion 1838 – 1927*, Marion, Iowa, Students of Marion High School; 1st Edition edition, 1995.

Taylor, Sue, *Grant Wood's Secrets*, University of Delaware Press, Newark, Delaware, 2020.

Rinard, Park, Secretary to Grant Wood, as dictated circa 1935 – 1940, *Return from Bohemia: A Painter's Story*. (Unpublished, though a copy is now included in Sue Taylor's *Grant Wood's Secrets*, published 2020.)

Wright, Mabel Osgood and Coues, Elliot, *Citizen Bird/Scenes from Bird-Life in Plain English for Beginners*, 1897. (No longer in print, but available electronically by demand.)

NON-PRINT SOURCES:
Grant Wood Scrapbook #74, as collected by sister Nan Wood Graham, University of Iowa Collection housed in Figge Art Museum, Davenport, Iowa, 1900–1964.

www: asphistory.com/Prison History Website, Anamosa, Iowa USA

Credits:

Pg. 55: Anamosa Prison and Prison Farm photos are by Barbara Feller.
Pg. 56: Photos of school, sign, and home by Steve Feller.
Pg 57: Cedar Rapids home, photo by Steve Feller.
Pg 58: Hattie Weaver Wood, c. 1930, by an unidentified photographer. Figge Art Museum, City of Davenport Art Collection, Grant Wood Archive (SB4). Grant Wood, *Woman with Plants*, 1929. Oil on Upsom board; 20 1/2 x 18 in. (52 x 46 cm.). Cedar Rapids Museum of Art, Iowa, museum purchase (31.1).
Pg 59: Hattie Weaver, c. 1874, by an unidentified photographer. Figge Art Museum, City of Davenport Art Collection, Grant Wood Archive (SB4)
Pg 60: Francis Maryville Wood, 1875. Figge Art Museum, City of Davenport Art Collection, Grant Wood Archive (SB4).
Pg 61: John "Jack" Wood and Grant Wood, c. 1900, by an unidentified photographer, Figge Art Museum Archive, City of Davenport Art collection, Grant Wood Archives (SB8).
Pg. 62: Grant Wood aged 10, photograph from the collections of Joan Liffring-Zug Bourret, Cedar Rapids Museum of Art.

Cover:
Grant Wood, *Spring in the Country*, 1941. Oil on Masonite; 24 x 22 1/2 in. (61 x 57 cm.) Cedar Rapids Museum of Art, Iowa, museum purchase (93.12). Used by Permission.

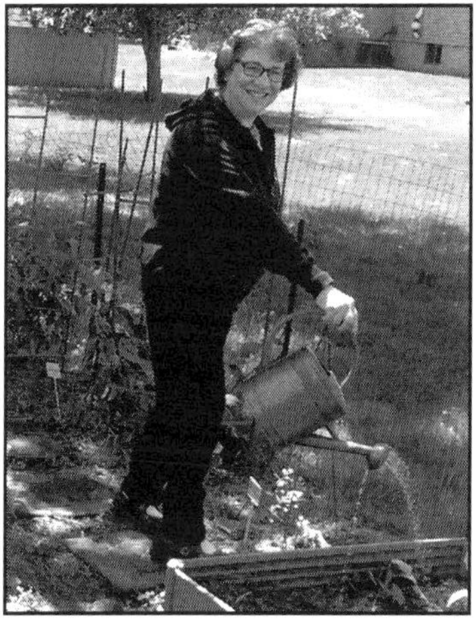

Born in the Bronx and raised in upstate New York, author Barbara Feller fell in love with Iowa and Iowans while working as an educator in area schools and museums. A part time teacher at Temple Judah since 1979, Barbara retired from her more public museum venue in 2013 with a desire to share inspiring stories of the history of her adopted community.

When not teaching or writing, Barbara tries to keep up with husband Steve, daughters Heidi and Ray, sons-in-law Howard and Michael and four incredible grandchildren: Max, Isaac, Leonardo, and Ramona.

Barbara has traveled extensively and enjoys gardening, reading, and cooking in her quieter moments.

Barbara is a member of the Wednesday Shakespeare Club, Martha Marquis Book Club of Coe College, and SCBWI (The Society of Children's Book Authors and Illustrators).

Barbara's earlier work, *Road to Waubeek: Discovering Jay G. Sigmund* and this new offering, *Creation of an Artist: A Story of Grant Wood's Childhood*, are available at IceCubePress.com.

The Ice Cube Press began publishing in 1991 to focus on how to live with the natural world and to better understand how people can best live together in the communities they share and inhabit. Using the literary arts to explore life and experiences in the heartland of the United States we have been recognized by a number of well-known writers including: Bill Bradley, Gary Snyder, Gene Logsdon, Wes Jackson, Patricia Hampl, Greg Brown, Jim Harrison, Annie Dillard, Ken Burns, Roz Chast, Jane Hamilton, Daniel Menaker, Kathleen Norris, Janisse Ray, Craig Lesley, Alison Deming, Harriet Lerner, Richard Lynn Stegner, Richard Rhodes, Michael Pollan, David Abram, David Orr, and Barry Lopez. We've published a number of well-known authors including: Bill Moyers, Mary Swander, Jim Heynen, Mary Pipher, Bill Holm, Connie Mutel, John T. Price, Carol Bly, Marvin Bell, Debra Marquart, Ted Kooser, Stephanie Mills, Bill McKibben, Craig Lesley, Elizabeth McCracken, Derrick Jensen, Dean Bakopoulos, Rick Bass, Linda Hogan, Pam Houston, and Paul Gruchow. Check out Ice Cube Press books on our web site, join our email list, Facebook group, or follow us on Twitter. Visit booksellers, museum shops, or any place you can find good books and support true honest to goodness independent publishing projects so you can discover why we continue striving to "hear the other side."

Ice Cube Press, LLC (Est. 1991)
North Liberty, Iowa, Midwest, USA
Resting above the Silurian and Jordan aquifiers
steve@icecubepress.com
check us out on twitter and facebook
www.icecubepress.com

To Fenna Marie
an artist in all ways
To Ingrid
a living work of art

Praise for *The Creation of an Artist*

"*The Creation of an Artist: Grant Wood's Boyhood Story* is a delightful short biography of Iowa's most famous artist. Directed at younger readers, the book will also be informative for all ages."—Joni Kinsey, PhD, author, "Cultivating Iowa: An Introduction to Grant Wood," in *Grant Wood's Studio: Birthplace of American Gothic, edited by Jane Milosch, 2005*

"Barbara Feller's warm and charming account of the first decade of artist Grant Wood's life in *The Creation of an Artist* was a joy to read. Thoroughly researched, the author takes the reader back to Wood's boyhood home near Anamosa, Iowa, using the sounds, symbols and language of this rural heritage. She also provides hints of the artist Wood is destined to become, exploring both his dreams and fears as he enters a new way of life in the much larger city of Cedar Rapids. The book is easy reading for all ages and a wonderful way to discover more about the formative years of Iowa's favorite artist."—Paul C. Juhl, author, *Grant Wood's Clear Lake Summer; Grant Wood: Abandoned Plans*; and *Grant Wood and Iowa State Fair*

"Barbara Feller's *The Creation of an Artist* artfully weaves together primary sources and engaging prose to illuminate the all-important early years of Grant Wood's life. If, as Wood himself once claimed, 'we're conditioned in the first twelve years of our lives,' then this exploration of the artist's childhood provides a valuable context for his often enigmatic work."—R. Tripp Evans, Professor, History of Art Co-Chair, Department of Visual Art and History of Art Wheaton College, Norton, MA

"*The Creation of an Artist: Grant Wood's Boyhood Story* paints an evocative picture of time and place in Iowa at the turn of the twentieth century. Feller's well-researched and engagingly told book is a sweet, thoughtful examination of the early years of Iowa's preeminent artist."—Katherine Kunau, Associate Curator of Collections and Exhibitions Cedar Rapids Museum of Art

"*The Creation of an Artist* captures the innocence and spirit of a ten-year old Grant Wood who is discovering his talent for becoming an artist. Barbara Feller's literary descriptions of Iowa, and its landscapes, at the onset of the 20th century, weave an inspiring story of family, heart and home. It made me want to go back home to Iowa, even if it's just for a day."—Dorothy Bunting Montgomery, author, *Stone Fruit*

"Discovering Grant Wood's early days gives us an insight on what was to follow."—Bill Thomas, a long-time local historian, volunteer guide, and Grant Wood's paper boy